Inside the Books

Readers and Libraries
Around the World

Toni Buzzeo

Illustrations by Jude Daly

UpstartBooks

Madison, Wisconsin
www.upstartbooks.com

*I love to look
inside the books.*

They beckon me
from wooden shelves
that guard the stories
hidden there ...

The United States
of America is on
the continent of
North America.

Many American
cities, towns,
and villages have
libraries large or
small.

A girl, a boy,
a special toy,
a wise and gentle
little bear.

I love to look
inside the books.

They glide within
a floating boat
to take me somewhere
strange and new …

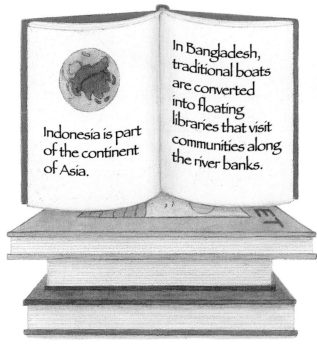

Indonesia is part of the continent of Asia.

In Bangladesh, traditional boats are converted into floating libraries that visit communities along the river banks.

A wooden skiff
or sailing ship

with fearless captain
and brave crew.

*I love to look
inside the books.*

They soar above
our frozen bay
and land with stories
cozy warm …

Antarctica is the world's coldest, driest, and windiest continent.

People who live there work at research bases. Esperanza Station on Hope Bay includes families, a community library, and a school with a library, too.

The southern lights
on winter nights,
and downy penguins
newly born.

*I love to look
inside the books.*

They nestle in
a donkey cart
and transport me both
near and far …

Ethiopia is on
the continent of
Africa.

Six donkey mobile
libraries, part of
the Ethiopia Reads
program, carry
books from school
to school and
village to village.

A mountain high,
a desert dry,

a rock-carved church
and ancient stars.

*I love to look
inside the books.*

They bump along
in wheelbarrows
with noble tales from
long ago …

England is part of
the continent of
Europe.

Using a
wheelbarrow,
assistants from
the Blackpool
Beach Library
deliver books to
people relaxing
on the sand.

A fearsome knight,
a castle bright,
a kingdom sparkling
in the snow.

*I love to look
inside the books.*

They perch within
a silent train,
their stories rumbling
to be heard …

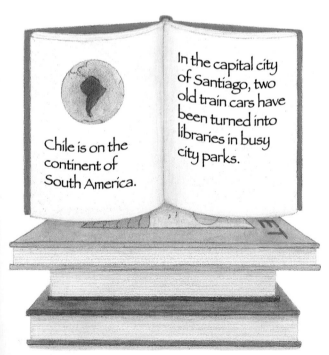

Chile is on the
continent of
South America.

In the capital city
of Santiago, two
old train cars have
been turned into
libraries in busy
city parks.

An Inca king,
folktales to sing,
rodeo riders
swift as birds.

*I love to look
inside the books.*

They cruise inside
a bright blue truck
and show our future
yet to be ...

Australia is the
world's only
country that is
also a continent.

Semi-trailer
trucks pull mobile
libraries, like the
Lake Macquarie
City Library
Mobile, to distant
places.

Green power flows,
our gardens grow,

protected species
thrive in trees.

I love to look inside the books.

They open worlds
I've never known,
bring friends and strangers,
sights to see.

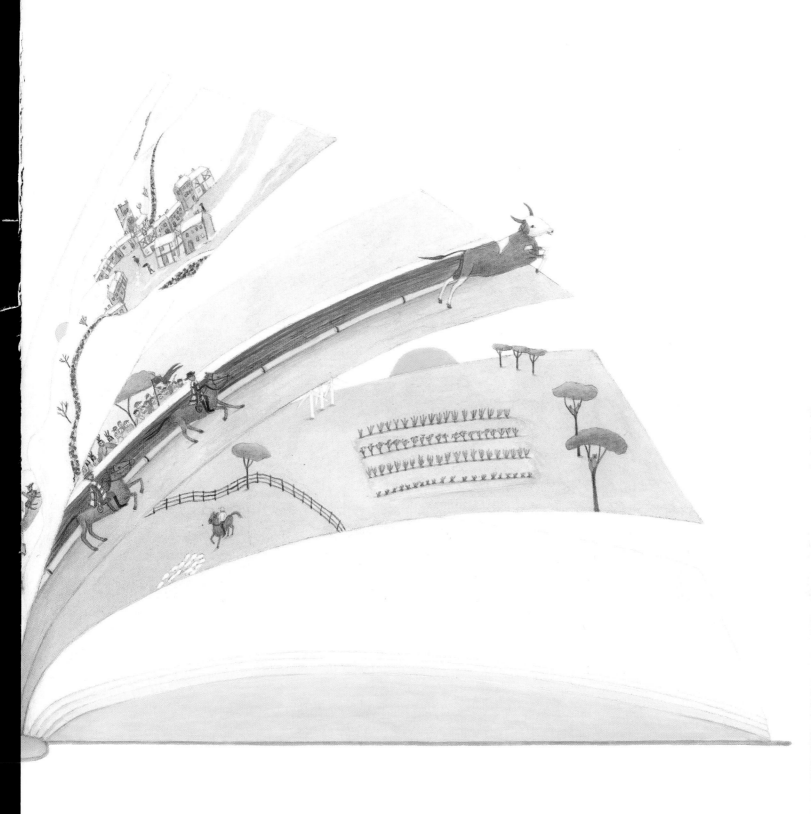

Books line the shelves.
We help ourselves.
All libraries share with
you and me.

*To children's librarians around the world who bring
the magic of books and stories to young readers—
and to Kelly Loughman, who helped me bring
magic to the pages of this book.*
—T. B.

For Leo & Magriet, with love.
—J. D.

Special thanks to the GLOBE Program (Global Learning and Observa-
tions to Benefit the Environment) and Escuela Provincial No. 38 Julio A
Roca, a GLOBE school in Esperanza, Antarctica. *www.globe.gov.*

Published by UpstartBooks
4810 Forest Run Road
Madison, Wisconsin 53704
1-800-448-4887

Text © 2012 by Toni Buzzeo
Illustrations © 2012 by Jude Daly
The paper used in this publication meets the minimum requirements of American National
Standard for Information Science — Permanence of Paper for Printed Library Material.
ANSI/NISO Z39.48.